Appointing and Managing Learning Support Assistants

A Practical Guide for SENCOs and other Managers

Jennie George and Margaret Hunt

 David Fulton Publishers

David Fulton Publishers Ltd
The Chiswick Centre, 414 Chiswick High Road, London W4 5TF

www.fultonpublishers.co.uk

First published in Great Britain in 2003 by David Fulton Publishers
10 9 8 7 6 5 4 3 2 1

David Fulton Publishers is a division of Granada Learning Limited, part of Granada plc.

British Library Cataloguing in Publication Data
A catalogue record for this book is available from the British Library.

ISBN 1–84312–062–3

Typeset by FiSH Books
Printed and

Contents

Acknowledgements

This book has been developed from the authors' work in training and supporting learning support assistants (LSAs) for the Local Education Authority in Bristol. With the revised Code of Practice making particular reference to the SENCO's role in managing LSAs (5.32), a set of training materials was prepared as part of Bristol's Continuing Professional Development programme and then delivered by the authors to the SENCO Cluster Support Groups across the city. Those materials form the basis of this book.

The authors would like to give a special thanks to Angela White, Deputy Head of Connaught Primary School, who was involved in the initial training day from which this book has grown.

TA or LSA?

There has recently been a move to refer to all additional adults working in schools as teaching assistants. However, as this book has been written for SENCOs who are managing additional support for pupils with special educational needs, the authors are using the term 'learning support assistants' as referred to in the Code of Practice (6.35).

N.B. Throughout the book, SENCOs are referred to as 'he' and learning support assistants as 'she'. This is not to suggest a gender bias in either role, but is used merely as a way of improving fluency in the text.

Introduction

Learning support assistants are increasingly being employed in schools as part of a professional team to support both pupils and teachers. The impetus for this change has come from several factors including:

■ the inclusion of children in mainstream schools who would have previously been educated in specialist provision, linked with the growth in numbers of pupils formally identified with special educational needs;

■ the push to raise standards in education: the vision for the future laid out in the Labour Education Manifesto (2001) asked for 20,000 new LSAs to be recruited, with the somewhat contentious suggestion that they have a bigger part to play in the teaching role including supervising groups and classes when teachers are absent; and

■ Local management of schools, which has given schools more control over their own budgets and made them more aware of financial constraints – the recruitment of LSAs seems to be very cost-effective.

The Cornerstones approach

Historically, there has been no formal route to becoming an LSA, or any career structure for individuals once in the role. Training has tended to be provided in a piecemeal way, with some schools and LEAs doing much more than others. Experience and 'learning on the job', coupled with attendance at occasional courses, have been the order of the day. The whole area of training and qualifications is being expanded as this book goes to print (see pages 46–7), but it remains incumbent on the SENCO to identify the personal strengths and training needs of his own particular team in order to maximise its effectiveness and provide high-quality support within the school.

LSAs will bring a range of personal skills and qualities to their roles which will need to be matched to specific duties wherever possible. As SENCO, you will be instrumental in identifying these strengths and providing opportunities for development in areas that are not so strong. The Cornerstones approach offers SENCOs a system with solid foundations on which to build a strong team. Each Cornerstone is essential in its own right but can only be truly weight-bearing when used with the other three.

Effective deployment – ensuring that the skills of the LSA match the needs of the pupil and school: the support is targeted to give maximum learning opportunities and curricular access.

Professional support systems – ensuring that LSAs are supported in their roles and have opportunities for professional development.

Communication – ensuring that there is an effective system in place whereby information flows freely between all relevant parties.

Monitoring the overall effectiveness of LSA support – ensuring that the support is having a positive impact.

The relationship between LSA and teacher/pupil/SENCO can be fraught. In Box 1 are some of the most often-cited concerns.

Box 1

If, as SENCO, you use the Cornerstones approach, there will be less opportunity for these issues to arise. Each of these will be explored in more detail later in the book. However, before moving on, it is necessary to ensure that you are clear about the current strengths and weaknesses in the support and management of LSAs in your school. In Chapter 1, we set out a framework for auditing your existing practice.

An audit of existing practice

In the day-to-day business of getting on with the job, responding to immediate situations and trying to keep up with the paperwork, it can be difficult to establish just what is going on in terms of pupil support; who is doing what, when and with whom? The issue of 'why' things are done in certain ways at certain times may be addressed only in times of extreme measures such as the run-up to an Ofsted inspection. In a busy school, this can lead to a lack of cohesion and diminishing returns in terms of measurable effectiveness. Time taken to conduct a careful audit of support will provide useful information for a SENCO which will form the basis for future decision-making and planning. The pro forma sheets on pages 6–7 may be useful.

Think about what is happening in terms of:

- Policy – Does the SEN Policy clearly indicate when, where and how LSAs will be deployed and how resources will be allocated?

- Roles and responsibilities – Are the LSA's roles clearly defined? Are all teachers clear about their roles and responsibilities in relation to the LSAs?

- An induction/mentoring system – is there one in place?

- Type of support – List and define – one-to-one teaching, small-group work (inside/outside the classroom), in-class support (directed at specific children/general).

- Programmes of support – Which specific programmes are used? Catch-ups, e.g. ALS, ELS Springbase Commercial packages, Phonographix, PAT. How many children are involved? Are these programmes part of the pupils' IEPs?

- Planning and liaison time – Do teachers hold responsibility for overseeing programmes – if not, who? Is there time for liaison? Is there time for preparation/resource-making? Is time set aside for teachers to share lesson plans?

- Assessment/monitoring (both of children and of LSA effectiveness) – What are the procedures for monitoring? Who monitors? How often? What happens to the information? How are children assessed and by whom? Does this information inform planning?

- Logistics – Where are LSAs working? Is there a timetable that guarantees a room/space to work with no interruptions? Is this space near the class to avoid wasting time on travel?

■ Resources – Are there enough for each LSA? Do LSAs have their own personal space to store resources? Where are shared resources located and what system is there for knowing who has what?

An example of a completed audit (Form 2) is provided on pages 8–9, and Form 3 (pages 10–11) describes how one SENCO planned for change.

School audit of LSA deployment

Date:...

Policy/rationale for deployment

Up-to-date job description/roles/responsibilities

Induction/mentoring

Type of support (i.e. group etc.)

Form I continued

Programme of support
Planning
Monitoring (both of children and of effectiveness of support)
Logistics – Where are they working?
Resources

Form 2

This is what one school found

Policy/rationale for deployment

School policy in place but not an effective working document. Areas of practice in the school not in line with policy, particularly in terms of criteria for LSA support.

Job descriptions/roles and responsibilities

No system for regular review and update of job description.
Current descriptions do not reflect the changing roles of the LSAs.
Responsibilities unclear.
New staff still being appointed on existing job descriptions.

Induction/mentoring

No established system for induction. Ad hoc arrangements heavily reliant on the LSA 'finding out'.
Written information available only through the parent handbook.
No specific handbook for LSAs.
LSAs often feel isolated when dealing with the most challenging pupils and 'guilty' if they perceive themselves as failing to control/change the pupil behaviour.

Type of support

Mainly 1:1 or small-group work with children withdrawn from class. Timetabling means children are missing out on direct teaching opportunities or other situations from which they could have benefited.
Children not accessing a broad and balanced curriculum.

Form 2 continued

Programmes of support

Programmes used depending on teacher's preference and LSA training. Evidence that some LSAs needed training in both literacy and numeracy techniques. No consistency in planning for different year (with the exception of ALS). Programmes not always age appropriate.

Planning and liaison time

No current planning patterns class by class. No time set aside for liaison. LSAs not always involved in target setting/reviews for IEPs. LSAs moving between classes not always told about the learning objectives.

Monitoring and assessment (both of children and of effectiveness of support)

Main responsibility for the monitoring of targets lies with the LSA. Monitoring not focused. Tendency for a narrative of events rather than how and what the child has learnt in relation to the specific target.

No system for effectively reviewing information held in the monitoring.

Children not involved in their learning objectives/planning.

LSAs not trained.

Overall, findings are: lots of hard work but no concrete information or indication of its impact on either raising attainment or developing inclusion.

Logistics – Where are they working?

Not enough designated space near the classroom. LSAs wasting time looking for a 'home' and can be displaced by more important happening, e.g. SMT meeting, school nurse etc., sometimes with no warning.

Furniture inappropriate for size of pupils, e.g. low coffee table and high chairs.

Also some corridor working which is very distracting for the children.

Resources

With exception of ALS materials, each LSA had own, mostly homemade equipment.

LSA not always choosing appropriate materials.

LSAs do not have either a personal or shared space in which to work.

Form 3

How the SENCO planned for change

Initial planning against audit information

Date:...

Area	Action
Policy/rationale for deployment	Policies to be implemented fully, not just on paper. Deployment and resource allocation to be working on the ground.
Job description/roles and responsibilities	Need for clarity of roles and responsibilities – to include LSA's input when planning IEP targets. System for regular review of job description linking with annual personal development interviews to be set up.
Induction/mentoring	LSA induction pack and handbook to be developed. Mentor to be identified for each new LSA. Opportunities for LSAs dealing with difficult children to have time to 'unload' by talking it through with an experienced member of staff.
Type of support (i.e. group etc.)	System of small-group/1:1 work needs further investigation and other models explored. Whole-school review on withdrawal vs. inclusion needed to take place.
Programmes of support	Suitable remediation/catch-up programmes to be introduced with training as appropriate. A provision map to be drawn up to show which programmes are being used for which year group.

Form 3 continued

Planning and liaison time	LSA working with individual pupils needs to be part of IEP target setting process. Time for planning/liaison to be built into existing LSA hours or more hours paid for. Pupil involvement!
Monitoring (both of children and of effectiveness of support)	Monitoring of targets to be revamped with training for LSAs involved. 'Before and after' assessment to show which programme most effective in results to be explored and cost. Pupil involvement!
Logistics – Where are they working?	Timetable to be set up for allocation of space with no changes. Time to be allowed for LSAs to move between groups.
Resources	Resources to be rationalised and extra space made for LSA's boxes and other equipment to ease accessibility.

Form 4

Following an audit of your own school make an initial plan of action

Initial planning against audit information

Date:...

Area	Action
Policy/rationale for deployment	
Job description/roles and responsibilities	
Induction/mentoring	
Type of support (i.e. group etc.)	
Programmes of support	

Form 4 continued

Planning	
Monitoring (both of children and of effectiveness of support)	
Logistics – Where are they working?	
Resources	

2 Communication

Communication with the LSA begins with her appointment to the school. The head and governors have a responsibility to ensure that *all* staff are aware of school policies. An LSA handbook is a useful way of providing all the information needed initially. On a practical level, a large ring binder, which enables information to be added/changed, is a good format.

Handbook for LSAs

A handbook could be laid out in sections with information relevant to each individual school setting.

Part I

Basic information about the school, which could include:

- copy of the school prospectus for general information;
- timetable of the school day (including breaks);
- school calendar for the current year, including holidays dates, staff meetings and training days etc.;
- how information is communicated around the school;
- location of materials, equipment and access arrangements;
- computer access arrangements;
- staff list;
- LSA timetable and room allocations; and
- information on any national/local initiatives relevant to the school.

Part 2

Roles and responsibilities, which could include:

- copy of accurate job description with working hours clearly set out;
- named person for induction/mentoring (to be inserted for each LSA);
- information about roles and responsibilities within school including SENCO; and
- school governors, subject coordinators etc.

Part 3

Policy and practice, which could include summaries of school policy documents on the following (with clear information about how these should be reflected in the LSA's daily work):

- special needs
- behaviour management and discipline
- equal opportunities
- health and safety
- first aid
- PE
- working in partnership with parents
- guidelines on confidentiality
- child protection and procedures for disclosure
- whole-school policy in areas such as handwriting, spelling
- the school's response to the Disability and Discrimination Act 2002.

Part 4

Details on procedures, which could include:

- dealing with visitors (signing in, badges); and
- notifying sickness/absences.

Part 5

Guide to working practices, which could include:

- information on monitoring IEPs, including worked examples and pro forma;
- information on expected involvement in review;
- pro forma and example of a short report for an annual review in case of support for a specific pupil; and
- directions on where belongings/resources can be kept safely.

Part 6

Professional development and training, which could include:

- information on professional development interview cycle;
- a copy of the interview pro forma with information on how it will be filled out; and
- information sheets on the high-incidence needs the LSA will meet, e.g. dyslexia.

Part 7

Other professionals involved in school – who they are and what they do, which could include:

- central support services – specialist support teachers for cognition/ communication and interaction/behaviour/sensory and physical impairment;
- educational psychologist;
- educational welfare officers;
- health professionals, e.g. speech therapists/occupational therapists/school nurse; and
- social workers.

LSA induction

Induction is an important process. People who receive a good induction into their new post will gain confidence and work more effectively. An induction policy should set out the rationale and procedures for all staff. This should include time to:

- observe the classes they will be supporting;
- talk to teachers about class rules/expectations;
- be trained in monitoring targets (if appropriate); and
- be introduced to parents/carers if they have undertaken 1:1 support.

The following checklist is a basic reminder of all the points that will help the LSA to get to know the school and to make a good start in her new job. Starting a new role can be daunting; there is a lot to take in and the LSA may be nervous. It will help to provide her with an opportunity to go over the information provided – after an interval of a few days – and ask any questions. The list on page 18 may help the LSA to remember points she needs to cover.

Form 5

Checklist for LSA induction

Name of LSA:.. **Mentor:**..

Date:..

Does the LSA have a job description and clear guidelines of duties? ☐

Has time been allocated for the LSA to discuss: induction package/induction programme with the mentor? ☐

Has the LSA been introduced to:

   all teaching staff, non-teaching staff and caretaker? ☐

   special needs advisory support teacher, school nurse, educational psychologist? ☐

   other professionals who may be involved with children the LSA supports? ☐

   parents, if appropriate? ☐

Have the following been discussed with the LSA?

   door codes ☐

   school timetable/personal timetable ☐

   holiday dates ☐

   breaktime arrangements ☐

   start-of- and end-of-day arrangements ☐

   lunchtime arrangements ☐

Other issues

Does the LSA know where to store resources? ☐

Have the following been discussed?

   Behaviour Management Policy ☐

   Health and Safety Policy ☐

....

....

....

....

Form 6

Checklist for learning support assistants

Are you clear about your role with the child/children you are supporting through discussions with the class teacher? ☐

If you are likely to have to deal with any emergency situations, e.g. if the child you are supporting has epilepsy, diabetes, temper tantrums, are you clear about the procedures you would take? ☐

If you are working with a child with a Statement, have you seen the Statement of Special Educational Needs? ☐

Are you confident about your role regarding keeping records and how these should be kept? ☐

Are you clear about your role in review meetings? ☐

Have you a regular time to meet with the class teacher to discuss your work with the children? ☐

Are you clear about your role regarding other children in the class (e.g. if asked to work with other or a group of children)? ☐

Are you clear about what your role is regarding discipline in the classroom? ☐

Do you know who you can go to in school if you have any concerns? ☐

Do you know who you can contact in the LEA if you have any problems, e.g. pay, contract, your own welfare, grievances, general advice? ☐

Do you have a place to keep your resources? ☐

Are you clear when your tea and lunch breaks are? ☐

Do you know what to do in the event of a fire? ☐

In what areas would you like training/guidance?

Ongoing communication

The LSA needs to have clear information about the school and her role within it, with access to an effective updating system. It must be clear whose responsibility it is to update LSAs with any changes that are taking place or any new information that is relevant to them. Assistants should be present at staff meetings where appropriate, though contracts differ in terms of how they are paid for 'non-contact' time, and this may impact on their willingness to attend. As many LSAs work on a part-time basis, there may also be childcare arrangements to consider; it can be more convenient and practicable to gather together all LSAs in a school for a separate meeting over a lunchtime, e.g. to update on whole-school issues.

There needs to be a triangle of communication between (a) the LSA and class teacher; (b) the LSA and SENCO; and (c) the class teacher and SENCO.

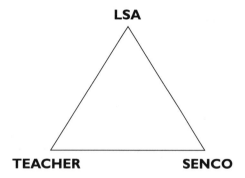

The teacher and the LSA

Successful working relationships are based on a clear understanding of roles and systems within the classroom. The LSA will need to know, for every lesson or group session, the teaching objectives for the children she is supporting. In return, the LSA will be able to provide the teacher with invaluable information on how the children approached the task and the progress they made. We have included on pages 21–24 examples of monitoring sheets for group work. These could be used either for monitoring 'catch-up' programmes or for group support as part of differentiation within a class lesson. It is therefore essential that quality time is allocated for the teacher and LSA to plan together. Leaving it to chance meetings over coffee or a snatched few minutes here and there will not only mean that support is ineffective but also that the LSA may come to feel devalued and disempowered.

When providing support at School Action, School Action Plus and with statements, the LSA should be fully involved in target setting for individual pupils and be trained in effective monitoring of IEP targets if they are undertaking these responsibilities. There is more information about monitoring in Chapter 5.

The following is designed as a checklist for all teachers but can be especially useful for NQTs and returning staff where it could form part of a teacher's induction pack.

The teacher and the LSA in partnership

Setting the scene

- Discuss with the LSA what work you will be expecting in your classrooms.
- Ensure the LSA has been taught to use teaching aids (e.g. computer) before she is expected to help a child.
- Ensure both you and the LSA are clear about your roles in whole-class teaching times, e.g. 'Big Book or mental maths'.
- Get to know the LSA, to ensure a good working relationship.
- Make the LSA aware of the class rules (e.g. going to the toilet, use of erasers etc.). These may differ from class to class.
- Ensure the LSA has a place in the classroom/cupboards to keep any equipment or personal belongings.
- Introduce the LSA to the children when appropriate and explain why she is there.

Planning

- Set aside specific time to discuss/plan together without interruption; ideally, this will be timetabled into the week. Have a weekly planning sheet where the LSA's tasks can be noted, and/or give the LSA your planning sheets with her role annotated and highlighted. A notebook can also be useful for jottings/reminders etc. when it is not possible to talk. Keep it somewhere where it is accessible to you both.
- Remember also that you prefer time to prepare before a lesson, so will the LSA.
- Plan work for/with the LSA and give clear guidelines.
- Make sure the LSA knows exactly what is wanted from the children and what are the learning objectives for each session. The LSA may not have been in the classroom when you were talking with them.
- Discuss in advance where, within the class, the LSA is going to work and make sure the space is available.

Other issues for your class

- ....
- ....
- ....

There will also need to be an effective feedback system on specific lessons/tasks, including monitoring group work, and on the following pages there are planning and ongoing monitoring sheets that can be adapted as running records.

Form 7

Planning and monitoring for group work

Pupil objectives:...

....

....

Date	Content	Comments	Actions

Individual pupil comments

....

....

....

....

....

....

Form 7a

Planning and monitoring for group work

Pupil objectives:......In-class support 'red group' ....

Following whole-class session on 'what is a mindmap'?

1. To demonstrate understanding of how mindmapping works.

2. To produce an individual mindmap using the theme 'books'.

Date	Content	Comments	Actions
4.6	1. Recap bases of mindmaps as taught to the whole class. 2. Generate ideas for 3 main branches in group discussion and chart. 3. Children decide on own central image and work with initial sub-branches.	Talking through ideas took longer than planned. Children haven't finished on their sub-branches, would like to continue in next session.	Check time available on Friday for finishing work.

Individual pupil comments

Evan – keen to contribute and managed to stay on-task for the whole session. Gave reward as in his Behaviour Plan. Don't think he actually realised he was working.

Kevin – very keen but found it difficult to come up with single words for his ideas – tried to describe everything in detail.

Todd – contributed lots of ideas, took a long time to draw his image.

Fran – only gave one idea, but has produced a map with main sub-branches and further branches that were not talked about so are all her own work.

Zoe – absent.

Form 8

Planning/monitoring sheets

Key learning points for the session

Activity:..

....

....

....

Resources needed:..

....

....

....

Key vocabulary to be emphasised:...

....

....

....

Monitoring outcomes

Name	Achieved ✓ Learning objectives	Needs further support Comment
....	I 2 3	....
....	I 2 3	....
....	I 2 3	....
....	I 2 3	....

Form 8a

Planning/monitoring sheets

Key learning points for the session

Activity:........Using Numicon Foundation Materials.......................................

1...To recognise plates 1–10...

3..To order plate 1–10...

2..To understand concept of 'one more', 'bigger'..

Resources needed:.........Red set – Card 7..

Numicon plates..

Numbers...

....

Key vocabulary to be emphasised:..........fast, next, one more, one less, biggest, bigger, last.

....

....

....

Monitoring outcomes

Name	Achieved ✓ Learning objectives	Needs further support Comment
Ricky	1 2 3	Needs to be directed to look carefully at plate. Muddled 678 order.
Sarah	1 2 3	Able to say 6 more than 5 and 10 more than 9.
Hamza	1 2 3	No difficulty putting plates in order. More support needed in terms of one/more/bigger.
	1 2 3	

The LSA and the SENCO

LSAs must also be included on a need-to-know basis if there are any particular issues for a child that may have direct impact on his behaviour or ability to access the curriculum. In recognition of this, integrity must be a key personal attribute of an LSA. The LSAs should have opportunities to raise concerns with the SENCO. Regular LSA team meetings (half-termly in contracted hours) can be an effective method. To keep the focus of the meeting, a joint agenda needs to be set in advance and a time-keeper appointed to ensure the meeting doesn't 'drift'. In some schools a 'sticking point' is presented by an LSA. This can be a description of a difficulty that the LSA is having with a pupil or group. The problem is then jointly solved. This has proved an excellent way of not only sharing experience and expertise, but also of creating a team feeling. Three examples are provided below.

Example 1		
	LSA:	'I'm timetabled to support the two Year 3 classes in the afternoons. I'm doing some small group work on numeracy in the space between the two classrooms in the corridor. It's the only place to go. Trouble is, the children get distracted because the others come out of the classroom to go to the toilet. Half the time I think it's only because they want to see what we're up to.'
	Suggestions from the group:	'Wouldn't it be better to try to do it in the classroom? You could have a corner and the others would know what you were doing, so it wouldn't bother you.' *Logistics can be difficult to solve; you may have to look at timetabling. Even if there are no easy answers the LSA will feel that her difficulties are being acknowledged.*

Example 2		
	LSA:	'When I'm working with Connor in Year 4, I have to take him to the annexe. It's a real struggle to get him there. He dawdles his way down the corridor, fiddles about, wants to touch everything. Sometimes it can take 10 minutes. Silly thing is, when he's there and got started he really gets on with it and says it's fun. It's turning into a pantomime.'
	Suggestions from the group:	'You could have a time card or sheet so he can "beat his own record" (no running though) and then have a reward. What about a special walkabout as a reward. Can't you work with him in the classroom? Why don't you try to do some of the "work" while you're walking – I-spy or something?' *Sharing problems like this one will generate a great many ideas. It will be your role as SENCO to decide which are appropriate.*

Example 3		
	LSA:	'I've got this Year 2 group and I'm doing high-frequency words. We're doing it "multi-sensory". I've used the wooden letters but I need some other ideas.'
	Suggestions from the group:	'Have you tried it with a feely bag?' 'I use changer pens; the children love those but you have to set the rules.' 'I've got a box of things like string and a bottle of sand.' *Sharing problems in this way often lead to a mini-project – in this case kitting out all the LSAs with a multi-sensory box of equipment.*

LSA, SENCO and class teacher – reviewing progress and setting new targets

The LSA working with individual pupils to support IEP targets will need to be involved in reviews and can be asked to make a written contribution to the annual review. To give the LSA a structure to work from, it is useful for her to have a pro forma. The following basic one can be added to meet the needs of your school.

Form 9

LSA report for individual child for annual review

Name:	D.O.B.:	Class Yr:

Input

Current IEP targets support
▪
▪
▪

Summary of evidence taken from monitoring sheets (including any test results)

Initial sounds: Symbol/sound: Sound/symbol:

High-frequency word-read: Spell:

Sequencing:

Pupil's comments

Signed:	Dated:

Form 9a

LSA report for individual child for annual review

Name: Carla	D.O.B.: 15.03	Class Yr: 2

Input

Input 5 x 20 minutes weekly on programme for literacy/language skills.
10 mins x 2 weekly pre-tutoring big book.
In-class support 1 hour daily during the Literacy Hour – targeted support.

Carla is beginning to make progress. She now knows most of her letter sounds and can segment and blend CVC words. She is beginning to want to write on her own and has a go at making up her own spellings if I prompt her and give lots of praise.

In the class she is getting much more confident. Since we have started the pre-tutoring for the 'big book' she is even putting her hand up to answer without being asked. When she is doing the group work she is much more willing to have a go although I still have to make sure she really understands what she is going to do and she often forgets. We have tried picture reminders but she doesn't want to be 'different'.

Carla's speech is now much clearer but she still has difficulty following instructions and sequencing events; she can get very muddled when she is trying to explain something, especially if she is excited about it.

Carla appears to enjoy working with me 1:1 and she is always ready to come out and work on the programme.

Current IEP targets support

- To say and write the sounds consistently.
- To read high-frequency words out of context: said, you, went, was, this.
- To be able to sequence a familiar story presented pictorially.

Summary of evidence taken from monitoring sheets (including any test results)

Initial sounds:	Symbol/sound: 23/26	Sound/symbol: 21/26

High-frequency word-read: 19   **Spell:** 14

Sequencing: Initially using up to 8 pictures to give the structure.
Now able to retell with average of 5 with minimal verbal prompts.

Pupil's comments

I like doing my work with Mrs Wright because she helps me. I like doing the 'silly story' game best.

Signed:	Dated:

Conclusion

In this chapter we have examined how good lines of communication will ensure not only that the LSAs will be able to work effectively, but that they will also be confident to ask for clarification, information and support when issues arise. We have made reference to the use of LSA team meetings and/or support groups as a vehicle for sharing problems and expertise and as a means of the LSA communicating her needs to you as SENCO. We have also emphasised the importance of the LSA working in partnership with the teacher, which includes regular exchanges of information and opportunities for joint planning and feedback.

In the next chapter we explore further how LSA expertise can be harnessed and enhanced through further professional development.

3 Professional support systems

Supporting pupils with special needs is a demanding role. In practice, some pupils often spend a great deal more time in direct contact with the LSA than they do with the teacher. This can only be effective if, in addition to the communication and deployment being right, there is also professional development for the LSA.

Professional development interviews and training opportunities should be offered to LSAs in the same way as they are to teachers. This is a two-way process enabling areas for development to be identified in terms of both the needs of the LSA and the school. There are a range of formats that can be used, and an example is provided in this chapter.

LSAs often deal individually with the most challenging pupils. Is there a clear system in school that enables the LSA to 'offload' some of the feelings she will inevitably hold at the end of a particularly difficult day? 'Supervision' – talking through difficulties with an experienced member of staff who will listen to and acknowledge the concerns and feelings of the LSA – has been found to be a supportive mechanism by some LSAs. If there is no-one in your school who can undertake this role, some Central Behaviour Support Services are able to offer this on a 'bought back' basis. Case conferencing, as already described, as part of a LSA team meeting can also support professional development and eliminate some feelings of isolation.

People work best when they feel valued. Praise is worth a lot but small things, like ensuring the LSAs have their own space to keep their personal possessions, can be excellent for morale. This is particularly important as many LSAs work in more than one area of the school. If you can find room for an LSA 'base', so much the better.

Identifying training needs

In identifying the training needs of the LSAs in your school you should use a range of mechanisms including:

- the professional development interview with the LSA;
- the priorities in the School Development Plan;
- the school response to the government initiatives;
- feedback from LSA support meetings (see above);
- the support required for specific high-level, low-incidence-needs children

as they join the school, e.g. pupils with a physical impairment or a specific difficulty such as Down syndrome. In these cases it is essential that all staff should receive training, not just the LSA who is supporting the child.

The professional development interview

Remember that interviews of any sort can be intimidating if not handled sensitively. Undertaking a professional development interview may be a new experience for you as a SENCO and you may feel slightly uncomfortable about the process especially in a small school where there are close personal working relationships. To make this a positive experience for both yourself and the LSA, you will need to consider the following:

- When will it happen and what time will you allow?
- Where will it be held?
- How will the process be managed?
- Why are you undertaking the interview?

When?

The interviewee needs to feel that the process is valued by the school; therefore, it should be undertaken during contracted hours or by arrangement with additional pay. The interview should be annual, but it is good practice to plan at least one short meeting during the year to review the process informally. If you have a newly appointed LSA, an interview after two terms may be appropriate.

Where?

The room should be private with a guarantee of no interruptions. Comfortable chairs, managed so that you are not sitting directly opposite the interviewee, and a low table are desirable.

How?

The LSA should be given a copy of the professional development pro forma at least two weeks before the date. This will help her to think about the areas that may be discussed and to take an active part in the discussion, rather than being 'put on the spot'.

And lastly, why?

The purpose of the interview must be clearly defined, i.e. a reason to celebrate achievement and an opportunity to plan for professional development. The focus of the interview should be on the positive aspects of the interviewee's contribution to the school. The areas for development need to be drawn out from the LSA, not be imposed in a judgemental way.

On the following pages you will find a pro forma with some specific guidelines for the interview itself and there is an additional prompt pro forma which you could give to the LSA prior to the first interview. Finally, there is a blank photocopiable pro forma for your own interviews.

Form 10

Professional development interview

Name:	
Post:	
Date:	

Summary of discussion

a. Things that have gone well (areas of work, development of skills etc.)

■ Choose 2 or 3 positive achievements, e.g. work with a difficult pupil, or a successful group. Give input from things you or others have noticed to show how important the work is.

■ Discuss the impact of a training course or school visit – how new skills have changed the way things are done.

b. Areas of less success/satisfaction: things that have been difficult

■ Try not to be too negative; look for positive things that have arisen from the experience.

■ Issues over pay and conditions, workload and relationships may arise here and may have to be passed to the head teacher or senior management team

■ Discuss ways of solving the above. What ideas has the LSA got to address the problem?

■ How can you help?

Form 10 continued

c. Areas of work/skills to develop

Consider the changes that might be taking place and the way LSAs are deployed. Do the LSAs need training or meetings set up to support them?

- Is there a spread of skills across the LSA team?
- What new skills would the LSA like to have?
- Useful to add outline of courses or training sessions to be considered.

d. Long-term career plans

Some LSAs may be thinking about teacher training or moving to a higher grade by going on higher education courses, or leaving to earn more money!

Form 10 continued

e. Professional development needs/interests for the year ahead

It is useful to take to the interview any latest local government information on LSA training that has come into school.

Consider training and availability for the LSA. She may have childcare issues, transport problems, or may need confidence-boosting support, if she has not effectively done any formal training.

f. Agreed actions

Draw together the points raised in the interview with any time constraints so that the review will take place after the actions have been completed.

Give a copy of the completed form to the LSA.

Review date:

Form 11

Professional development interview

Prompts for the LSA

Name:
Post:
Date:

Summary of discussion
a. Things that have gone well (areas of work, development of skills etc.)
Think of 2 or 3 things that you are pleased with: support for an individual child; a group that has made good progress; ideas from a course that you have put into practice. ■ *support for a group...* ■ *ideas to extend learning...* ■ *good feedback from a teacher;* ■ *a pupil who has made good progress, when you feel you have helped.*
b. Areas of less success/satisfaction: things that have been difficult
Consider a problem that has 'gone home' with you, that you have felt was beyond your control. *How did you begin to solve the problem?* *Is there anything the SENCO/class teacher/colleagues can do to help you, or does the head teacher need to be involved?*

Form 11 continued

---

c. Areas of work/skills to develop

■ Are you interested in extending your experience in special needs? Is there, for example, a specific child in your school you would like to work with?

■ Would you like to build up expertise in a particular area, e.g. dyslexia, autistic spectrum disorder, behaviour management?

■ Would you like to concentrate on a particular curriculum area?

■ Look at training courses available – does anything match your interest?

■ Think about something you would like to be better at – ICT skills perhaps.

■ Are you interested in undertaking an accredited course, e.g. NVQ?

---

d. Long-term career plans

Would you like to move on in the LSA career path, becoming, for example, a learning mentor, LSA manager or even think about teacher training?

Form II continued

---

e. Professional development needs/interests for the year ahead

With your SENCO identify any courses you would like to attend or visits you would like to make.

- neighbouring school/s
- behaviour support unit
- speech and language therapist.

Perhaps you and your colleagues have identified some 'in-school' issues about which you would like outside agency involvement.

Could an afternoon meeting be set up?

---

f. Agreed actions

Review date:

Form 12

Professional development interview

LSA preparation

Name:
Post:
Date:

Summary of discussion
a. Things that have gone well (areas of work, development of skills etc.)
b. Areas of less success/satisfaction: things that have been difficult

Form 12 continued

c. **Areas of work/skills to develop**

d. **Long-term career plans**

Form 12 continued

e. Professional development needs/interests for the year ahead

f. Agreed actions

Review date:

Observation

Teachers are now very familiar with the systems of observation to support professional development. The same principles that underlie this system – identifying and building on good practice and agreeing areas for development – can be used to support the professional development of LSAs.

Being observed can be a daunting experience unless it is made clear that this process is supportive and not judgemental. The following two pro formas could be used to record the observation and to form a basis for feedback.

Pro forma 1 is for a general observation. Pro forma 2 may be observed in 1:1/small-group with specific elements to be observed.

For any observation, background information regarding adequate liaison, explanation by the teacher of the task, expected outcomes and dynamics of the group must all be taken into consideration.

If there is evidence that the LSA has just been 'left to it' (the issues lie with classroom management and the teacher perception of the role of the LSA), this will need to be addressed directly through the teacher.

Allow time for the feedback and concentrate on the positives.

Form 13

Observation sheet

Name: ....

Date: ....

| Group support ☐ | In-class ☐ | In-class ☐ |
| 1:1 support ☐ | | Withdrawal ☐ |

Lesson observation

Context

What went well

Ideas to consider

Feedback/comments

Observer

LSA

Form 13a

Observation sheet

Name:...... Sarah Martin ....

Date:......... 22.11.02 ....

| Group support ☐ | In-class ☐ | In-class ☐ |
| 1:1 support ☐ | | Withdrawal ☐ |

Lesson observation

Context

Work with 3 x Yr 2 pupils on a 10-week catch-up programme. Lesson observed week 3, day 2.

What went well

Children clear about the purpose of the session.

Instructions clear and checks made that children understood tasks.

Resources well organised. Colour coding children's individual words ensured children were 'self-contained'.

The pace of the input was good.

Appropriate use of positive and specific praise.

Ideas to consider

You may find it useful to number under the letter to help Sam when word building with the whole group.

Save a couple of minutes at the end of the session for the children to reflect on what they had learnt.

Feedback/comments

Observer

Children all had a 'have a go' attitude which would indicate they feel they are in a safe learning environment.

LSA

Sarah felt the session had gone well; she felt more confident working with the programme after two weeks.

Observation of LSA support session

Year group	Number of pupils
Length of session	Focus of support
Was there adequate planning time with teacher?	Was there adequate time for preparation of: (a) Resources? (b) Work areas?

Areas for consideration/support

Effective behaviour management

Time management

Learning objectives clearly explained

Form 14 continued

Language adapted/modified to meet the needs of individual pupils

Independence being promoted

Recap of learning objectives – as the children know what they have learnt

Effective monitoring against IEP targets

Other positive observations

Feedback notes

Planning development

Once you have clearly identified areas for development, you will need, together, to explore routes to acquire these new skills. Together, you will also need to consider this in the context of the LSA's long-term career aspirations. The recent National Standards, together with the single status guidelines to LEAs, have enabled clear career routes to be defined.

The options for personal and professional development include:

Internal

- *In-house*
  Individual support, e.g. training carried out by a teacher, or 'buddying' with a more experienced LSA.

- *Whole group*
  If several LSAs have identified the same need, you could consider buying in specific training over one or more sessions, e.g. supporting literacy, promoting independence, supporting a child with ASD. Some authorities run traded specialist learning and behaviour support services that could provide this tailor-made to your needs. If your authority does not provide this facility you may be able to find a neighbouring authority that does. It can be a very cost-effective method of providing high-quality training.

External

- Visiting another school – buddy in another school.

- *LEA training programme*
  LEAs provide training opportunities through Continuing Professional Development programmes, many of which are open to LSAs. If you have not got one locally, again you may be able to tap into one provided by a neighbouring authority.

- *Accredited qualification*
  In 2001 the Local Government Training Organisation published the National Occupational Standards for TAs. These now form the basis of the NVQ Level 2 and 3 qualifications that are offered by some LEAs and many HE colleges.

  Your local university may provide training modules for LSAs which carry credits towards certificates, diplomas and degrees.

  There are distance learning courses available including some through the Open University.

Encouraging reflection on practice

An integral part of any knowledge based course will be the building of a learning log. Even if your LSAs are not undertaking accredited external training, a log related to their identified area of development may be a help for them to reflect on what they are learning as they undertake their day-to-day roles and responsibilities.

Additional information regarding qualifications etc.

For additional information about national accredited courses, contact your local higher education college. For general information on NVQs the following websites are useful:

www.cache.org.uk
Follow links for career information;

or

www.lg-employers.gov.uk/skills/teaching/
lg-employers is the local government employees training organisation which has produced the National Standards for NVQs and the values and principles that underpin them.

4 Effective deployment

As the role of the LSA becomes an integral part of a school's educational provision, the deployment of the LSAs should support pupils both to access the curriculum and to be included within the classroom setting. The criteria you use for deployment should be clearly set out in your school's Special Needs Policy.

Your main considerations will be:

- how to balance the need for in-class support with small-group and 1:1 withdrawal for specific teaching programmes;
- how to ensure a balance of support across the curriculum; and
- if the children are being withdrawn, how to support the teachers in ensuring that skills are not learnt in isolation and that they can be transferred into the classroom.

The key question is, Does the deployment foster dependence or independence?

Withdrawal vs. in-class support

Withdrawing pupils from the classroom has both advantages and disadvantages. On the plus side:

- the work can be tailored to the needs of the child. Specific skills can be broken down into small steps and work re-enforced;
- distractions can be minimised, but only if a suitable workplace can be guaranteed; and
- the older child will not feel exposed if he cannot grasp the concept immediately or is slower to complete tasks.

However, on the minus side:

- constant withdrawal can lead a child to feel isolated;
- unless carefully planned, the work can be out of context and skills are not always generalised;
- for children who are constantly withdrawn, there can develop a culture of dependence; and
- there is a loss of contact with more able children when research shows that it is beneficial for children with learning difficulties to work with more able pupils.

The effect on the self-esteem of the child should always be of paramount importance. There are children who spend the greater part of their primary school career in small groups 'catching up' or in 1:1 situations working on specific skills. For some there is the worst practice of withdrawal with no real focus.

Deployment to support the three-wave model of intervention

Both the Literacy and Numeracy Strategies emphasise the need to meet all pupils' needs and are advocating a three-wave model of provision.

Wave 1

Whole-class teaching, which is appreciated.

Wave 2

Specific small-group catch-up programmes including, where appropriate, social skills.

Wave 3

Intensive work on specific skills including language.

As you will note LSA support is an integral part of this model.

At Wave 1

The LSA is a 'resource' that supports differentiation and ensures that pupils, whatever their needs, can access the tasks.

At Wave 2

LSAs can give direct instruction to small groups of pupils who can be expected to 'catch up' with their peers. It should be noted that as the children are expected to catch up, this is not primarily SEN provision. However, there may be pupils in these groups with identified special educational needs in other areas of behaviour or sensory impairment. The programmes should be structured with clear learning goals. Examples include those written in the strategies such as ELS/ALS or their commercially produced equivalents. It should also be noted that Wave 2 provision can include programmes to support the acquisition of skills that underpin literacy/numeracy, such as language programmes or programmes that will enable children to access whole-class teaching, such as social skills programmes.

The LSAs deployed to deliver these programmes will need:

- specific training in delivering the programmes;
- dedicated time to prepare resources;
- dedicated distraction-free workspace close to the classroom;
- time at the end of each session to write up monitoring notes; and
- time to liaise with the class teacher.

At Wave 3

These programmes should address the needs of pupils who have not made the expected progress at whole-class or catch-up stages. Although, ideally, children who need intensive work should be taught by a specialist teacher, in practice this role will often fall to the LSA. However, it should be emphasised that the programmes they are delivering should be prepared and monitored by a teacher or other specialists such as a language therapist, and that as the SENCO you will have a major role in supporting the LSA and overseeing the programmes.

Again, as with Wave 2, there is a need for specific ongoing training.

The choice of which waves the LSAs will be involved in will largely be determined by their experience, skills and training. The information gained through the Professional Development Cycle will inform your deployment decisions.

All of this would appear fairly clear cut; however, in addition to the three waves, you may also be deploying LSAs to support pupils with behaviour difficulties, sensory or physical impairments, or to support pupils with significant learning difficulties across the curriculum. There are two other important considerations which are especially important when deploying an LSA to undertake high levels of support for individual pupils with complex needs both in class and through withdrawal:

- Are the personalities comparable? Although there are often times when it is difficult to find an LSA at all, deploying someone who will give a wrong mix can be really counter-productive for the child and stressful for the LSA.

- Has the child been involved? He should be consulted. Consider what sort of help does he actually want. It should be explained who will be supporting him, why that person has been chosen, what the person will be doing/not doing and what the expected outcomes of the support will be. If this all sounds daunting, in practice it is a simple task and will stop the child being 'done unto'.

LSA timetables

You will need a clear overview of what each LSA is doing and it will also form the focus for discussion during professional development interviews and when job descriptions are reviewed. A simple sheet that sets out clearly the roles and responsibilities can form a useful record for both yourself and the LSA.

Form 15

Deployment record

Name of LSA:..

Term:.. **Date:**..

Whole-class support

Group work

Individual support

Other duties

Deployment record

Name of LSA:....... Lynne Seal ....

Term:....... Spring .... **Date:**.........4.01.03 ....

Whole-class support

3W Literacy Hour daily

Group work

Year 3	Structured spelling programme
Group 1	4 x 20 mins weekly 2 groups of 3
Azeem	
Michael	
Kimberley	

Individual support

Support for IEP	Motor control programme in liaison with
Sam Marcus Year 2	occupational therapist 20 mins daily

Other duties

Distribution of tuck to KS3 children -	8:45 – 9:00 am each day
Playground duty	
Key LSA supporting attendance -	Monday – Thursday 10:00 – 10:30 am
	Tuesday/Wednesday/Thursday 9:00 – 9:30 am

5 Monitoring effectiveness

As SENCO you will be monitoring the attainment of pupils who are at School Action, School Action Plus and with Statements of Special Educational Needs in relation to the attainment of their peer group. There is currently a range of data within schools that will enable you to establish these patterns of attainment. These include:

- end of key stage assessments in terms of National Curriculum levels;
- number of pupils at School Action, School Action Plus, a year-on-year comparison;
- number of pupils that do not make at least a one-level move in each of the core subjects over a key stage;
- number of pupils who show an increase on standardised reading or maths tests; and
- fixed-term exclusion rates.

By monitoring LSA support you will be able to maximise their effectiveness. This means monitoring the achievements of individual children both academically and socially. For children taking part in standard catch-up programmes such as ALS or ELS, attainment can be clearly charted, but how will you monitor the support where there is not such a strong 'script', e.g. for pupils with emotional or behavioural difficulties, language or communication impairments or physical impairments?

Whatever measurement you choose it should be based on positives. Your mantra should be: 'Is now able to ...'

Although some children will need to have ongoing support, the ultimate measure of effectiveness is the level of independence the children achieve. There have been occasions where LSAs have been 'attached' to a pupil in Year 1 or even earlier and have stayed with them throughout the primary phase. The role of the 'Velcroed' LSA can end up being counter-productive and there is a real danger that she will become so protective of the child that she will be doing the thinking for him; a case of who needs who most.

Questions to consider:

- What information will you use to monitor effectiveness?
- How and when will you collect and collate it?
- How will you build flexibility into the deployment to enable changes to be made?

When deciding what data to use to measure impact, you will also have to take into consideration some of the constraints attached to your choice.

IEP targets achieved in relation to input

This can be used for all areas including literacy, numeracy, language/communication and behaviour. Targets can also be set to foster independence and 'un-Velcro' the LSA. However, targets need clearly to identify the exact role and responsibility of the LSA and have measurable success criteria. If the LSA is responsible for part of the target she will also be responsible for monitoring the progress. This is not as easy as it would appear and you will need to ensure that appropriate training is given to avoid the end-result reading like a diary of the session rather than reflecting outcomes and the effectiveness of teaching strategies.

Involving the pupil

Pupils should not only be involved in setting targets but also in monitoring how they are progressing. Thought should be given to how this can be achieved. End-of-session recap on 'what I have learnt' will give additional insight into what a child feels he is achieving. For pupils with behavioural problems it is vital that they reflect on their targets at the time, e.g. to be able to come in and sit on the carpet – this could be monitored by the pupil with the LSA, and we have enclosed an example.

We are including here a short section on IEP monitoring which you could use as a basis for a training session with your LSA together with three photocopiable examples of monitoring sheets.

Monitoring IEP targets

Why monitor?

Progress needs to be monitored in order to:

■ ensure that the child can make progress, by letting everyone supporting the child know if the IEP targets or strategies are correctly set or will need adjusting before the next review;

- provide ongoing assessment, informing the teacher quickly if there is a deterioration or improvement, so that plans can be changed; and
- provide evidence of the provision being made, for accountability purposes.

Who monitors?

Monitoring arrangements should be set out and recorded when the IEP is drawn up, and say who will do what, when and how. For example:

'Class teacher will record any progress made on targets at end of each fortnight.'

'John will record the number of ticks received on his chart at the end of each week.'

'LSA will monitor progress within the programme weekly.'

Monitoring should usually be *overseen* by the same teacher who constructed the IEP, but a range of different people who are actually working with the child will contribute by jotting things down.

Monitoring will form an important element of annual reviews when rates of progress over the year against different strategies may be discussed.

How to monitor

There are many different ways of monitoring. All are acceptable as long as they fulfil the core purposes of monitoring as described and as long as they relate to the targets set out on the IEP, rather than describe the pupil's behaviour in general, or the teacher's lesson plan. Monitoring needs to record *significant* achievements rather than just what has been taught.

Monitoring needs to be against the targets. If, for example, the target is to learn to read X number of high-frequency words in context, it is those exact words that need to be monitored. A good IEP target will also set the success criteria which can make monitoring easier: '... will be able to read X high-frequency words in context on two successive occasions' gives a real handle to hang the monitoring on.

Progress monitoring summary sheet

Targets from IEP	
1.	
2.	
3.	
4.	

	1.	Target achieved
	2.	Measurable progress
	3.	No progress

Name: ....

Plan: .... Monitoring: ....

Date	Target	Remarks/comments	1.	2.	3.
		Summary			

Progress monitoring summary sheet

Targets from IEP

1.	To be able to segment and blend CVC words using the sounds both aurally and using letters a t f c o s.
2.	To read and spell the high-frequency words, went, this, like, me, said.
3.	To be able to count in 2s to 20 and 10s to 50.
4.	

1.	Target achieved
2.	Measurable progress
3.	No progress

Name: David **Plan:** 2 **Monitoring:** Fortnightly

Date	Target	Remarks/comments	1.	2.	3.
2.03.03	1	Aural: more confident with segmenting than blending – 'lost' the last sound when blending 3/6 times. Difficulty also holding last sound when building word with letter.		✓	
2.03.03	2	Enjoys the multi-sensory activities. Correct with – went like, me reading and spelling on last 3 successive occasions.	✓		
2.03.03	3	10s achieved – consistent on last 5 successive occasions. 2s unsure after 10.		✓	
	1				
	2				
	3				
		Summary			

Target monitoring behaviour group or individual

Name: ....

Week beginning: ....

Monday	Tuesday	Wednesday	Thursday	Friday

Target monitoring behaviour group or individual

Name: ....

Week beginning: ....

	Monday					Tuesday					Wednesday					Thursday					Friday				
	R	L	N	R	A	R	L	N	R	A	R	L	N	R	A	R	L	N	R	A	R	L	N	R	A
1. Sit for 5 minutes in carpet times, putting your hand up to speak.	:(	:|	:)	:(	:)	:(	:)	:)	:(	:)	:(	:)	:(	:)	:)	:(	:(	:)	:)	:(	:)	:)	:)	:(	
2. Come in to class in the morning and sit near Miss Cutmore with a book to read.	:)					:)					:)					:)					:)				
3. Sit on the carpet quietly waiting for Dad at 3:30.	:)					:)					:)					:)									

SEN monitoring sheet

Name:.. **SA/SA+Statement monitored by:**.......................................

Targets for week/month/term

1. ....

2. ....

3. ....

4. ....

Date	Target	Progress notes	Progress	Achieved

Form 18a

SEN monitoring sheet

Name:.. SA/SA+Statement monitored by:..

Targets for week/month/term

1. To tell a short story from a series of pictures (3 successive occasions) ....

2. On completing a short activity to say in order what he has just done (3 successive occasions)..............

3. ....

4. ....

Date	Target	Progress notes	Progress	Achieved
11/11	1	Have used 5-picture sets – needed lot of help/modelling. Will use 3-picture sets next week.		
11/11	2	Needed to model it carefully each time and use same objects/pictures.		
17/11	1	Found it much easier with 3 pictures and even able to add different ending with prompts – extend to 4.	✓	
17/11	2	Getting more confident, not ready to model but still using objects for prompts.	✓	

This chapter has highlighted the importance of monitoring by LSAs to support either individual pupils or small groups to show how their progress can be recorded and their needs met. We have asked questions of the LSA about recording information on the child's strengths, what the child is doing now, and the most recent measurable and observable information about the child. Has the child been set targets or objectives and are these targets achievable? The forms are examples of good practice developed over time by the authors and team members of the Learning Support Service for Bristol. They have all been used in schools supported by the team.

In the concluding chapter we give you suggested interview questions and tasks, plus references and website address you may find useful.

6 And finally...suggested interview questions and tasks

Increasing numbers of LSAs are being employed in schools. In the past it has often been a rather haphazard exercise involving friends of friends on short-term contracts without any formal interview or selection process.

To bring this book full circle we include suggested interview questions and scenarios plus tasks that could help you in this process.

Some suggestions for interview questions

The following suggestions have been compiled to assist you in devising interview questions. The list is not exhaustive. When actually asking the questions you may want to provide more context in order to make them less formal, e.g. 'We enjoyed reading your letter of application. Can you tell us a bit more about why you're interested in applying for this job?'

General questions

1. Can you tell us why you are interested in applying for this job?
2. Have you achieved success with anything recently that you'd like to tell us about?
3. What strengths could you bring to this school?
4. Tell us something about your experiences with children.
5. What skills can you bring to support the class teacher, e.g. art, music, IT?
6. Tell us a bit more about ... (select something from the letter of application; e.g. working with teenagers in a social setting, or as a playgroup leader)
7. We want to help our children become independent learners. If you are there as support, how will you ensure the pupil doesn't become dependent on you?

Supporting the academic curriculum

1. Sometimes pupils are given intensive support to develop literacy or numeracy. If you were asked to work with a group of children, what kinds of things do you think you would need to be told in order to have a successful session with them?
2. Children sometimes have difficulty in reading the instructions or information needed to complete a task. What do you see as your role in this situation?

Supporting the social curriculum

1. One of the pupils you would be supporting needs firm limits and boundaries. He will need to learn to follow classroom routines. How would you go about developing these?

2. What ideas do you have about maintaining a child's interest and concentration in a task directed by the teacher?

3. What ideas do you have about helping this child to develop play and/or friendship skills with other children?

4. What problems do you think a pupil with challenging behaviour might have in the ordinary lesson? How would you help him with those?

5. Why do you think pupils behave inappropriately in lessons?

6. If the target for a pupil was not to say something nasty or hurtful to the pupil next to him, what strategies would you use to help him to meet the target?

7. How would you manage the times when this pupil cannot cope, e.g.:
   - has a tantrum when he cannot get his own way?
   - tries to injure himself by banging his head against the wall?

8. How would you go about rewarding a pupil for good behaviour?

9. What kinds of behaviour by school staff do you think can help to develop a pupil's self-esteem?

10. What would you do to unwind if you have had a particularly challenging day?

Supporting a pupil's physical needs

1. The child is learning to use the toilet at appropriate times and we would expect that to be an early target. How would you go about developing this?

2. You know from the job specification that a pupil has diabetes/epilepsy. What do you know about diabetes and what would you do if he became unwell?

Managing group activities

1. How would you manage a group of children working around the school, e.g. six children collecting frogspawn from the conservation area?

2. How would you manage a group of four or five children playing an exciting reading game in the classroom?

3. While supporting a pupil's needs through classroom activities, how would you guard against the pupil becoming too reliant upon you?

   Or

   Give an example, specific to the pupil, e.g. 'K...has problems remembering a sequence of instructions given to the whole class. He is beginning to think that he doesn't have to attend to the teacher at all because someone will go through it all again with him.' How could you help?

4. What ideas do you have about helping the pupil to become as independent as possible?

Working as part of a team

1. You will be working as part of a team that includes other LSAs and teachers. Please tell us about a situation when you have worked as part of a team.
2. What qualities do you think are needed to be an effective LSA?

Training and the future

1. What would you like to be doing in, say, three years' time?
2. Are there any aspects of this job where you feel you would benefit from further training?

Relationship with parents/carers

1. We see the partnership with parents as very important. How do you see your role in that partnership?

Forming and maintaining relationships with the pupils

1. How would you go about making a relationship with the children you would be supporting? (If appropriate, give a focus, e.g. this pupil has a visual impairment.)
2. What ideas do you have about promoting a positive image about a child's needs:
   - in class?
   - in school?
   - in the community?
   while maintaining professional confidentiality.

Scenarios

1. The class teacher directs you to work with a group of pupils on a particular task. You quickly realise that the task is too difficult at this time. What would you do?
2. Children do occasionally use abusive language. How would you respond if a child told you to 'f...off'?
3. The class teacher is working with a group of children. You notice a child climbing up the door in a cloakroom. What would you do?
4. An adult rushes up to you and says that he has to take his child to the dentist. What do you do?
5. You are given a group to work outside the classroom. Three of the children have learning problems but one has real behavioural difficulties. What would you do?
6. At playtime you notice an adult standing in the playground/sitting in his car in the car park watching the children. What would you do?
7. The SENCO has asked you to use a particular programme with a pupil. The class teacher asks you to put up a display during the time you would normally have been working with this pupil. What do you do?

8. While you are shopping, a parent of a child at the school stops you and tells you that he doesn't want his child to sit by an EBD pupil you are supporting. How would you respond?

9. A parent stops you in the street and gets angry with you because you have had to discipline his child the day before. He thinks that you have been unfair. What do you say?

And finally...

1. Do you have any questions which you would like to ask us?
2. If you were offered the job would you accept it?
3. Where can we contact you and what is a convenient time?

Interview tasks

It is good practice to include a small task as part of the interview process. This could be either a prepared piece of work, or a task given on the day or out of the pack.

Here are some suggestions which have been used in schools:

1. The school is intending to set up a tuck shop at playtimes. You are asked to organise this. Make a plan of what you would need to do.

2. Give the candidate a pen-picture of a child. Discuss the school situations where the child might experience difficulties and what could be done to anticipate/help. An example might look something like this:

> Alan is a Year 5 boy who has a Statement. He is a friendly boy who wants to please and who gets on well with adults and other children. Working on the computer is one of his favourite activities. When instructions are given to the whole class, he finds it difficult to remember them for long enough to act upon them. He finds it difficult to learn new things and to retain information. He can write simple stories, but is still unsure of punctuation. He can be reluctant to answer questions during the Literacy or Numeracy hours because he is anxious about being wrong.

3. Write a note to a parent about, e.g. homework, in a pupil's planner.

4. Design a game to help a pupil learn to, e.g. spell selected word from a subject-specific word bank.

   Alternatively, you could:

5. Observe the candidate playing a game with a group of children. In this case there should be a chance for the candidate to meet the children before the observation and spend some time building a rapport.

Useful references and web pages

Useful references

For you as SENCO

Including All Children in the Literacy Hour and Daily Mathematics Lessons: Guidance on Management Issues for Headteacher, SENCO, Literacy and Mathematics Coordinator. (This includes section on three waves of provision and reviewing the roles of additional adult.) London: DfES. (Ref: 465/2002).

Index for Inclusion (2002). Tony Booth and Mel Ainscow. Available from CSIE, Room 2S203, S Block, Frenchay Campus, Coldharbour Lane, Bristol BS16 1QU.

Learning to Support: Training for Special Support Assistants (1997). Moira Challer and Kevin Major. In-service materials for assistants covering SEN – Ways of Working, Observation and Recording. Useful resource for in-house training/professional development. Bristol: Lucky Duck Publishing. www.luckyduck.co.uk

Multi-sensory Teaching: A Practical Guide to Multi-sensory Techniques (1994). Hugh O'Connell. A useful booklet outlining 'application resources and organisation'. www.desktoppublications.co.uk

SEN Coordinators File (published tri-annually). Practical support for all areas of SEN. Includes section on and for teaching assistants. London: PFP Publishing Ltd. www.pfp.publishing.com

The SENCO Handbook (4th edn) (2003). Elizabeth Cowne. London: David Fulton Publishers.

Working with Teaching Assistants: A Good Practice Guide (2000). London: DfEE (Ref: 148/2000).

For LSAs

A Handbook for Learning Support Assistants: Teaching and Assistants Working Together (2nd edn) (2003). Glenys Fox. London: David Fulton Publishers.

Supporting Literacy and Numeracy: A Guide for Learning Support Assistants (2000). Glenys Fox and Marian Halliwell. London: David Fulton Publishers.

Useful web pages

www.bda-dyslexia.org.uk/main/accreditation/lsa_course_guidance.asp
Information on accredited courses for LSAs and British Dyslexia Association.

www.national-inspections.co.uk
Under 'training for classroom assistants'. Includes latest section including useful tips/resources, together with a list of courses and workshops.

www.sw-special.co.uk
Supporting the supporter. Pages devoted to the work of learning support assistants, nursery nurses and mentors.

www.teachernet.gov.uk
Under 'most popular' select 'support staff'. Latest news on a range of issues including training.

Keep up-to-date with these SEN books from

 **David Fulton** Publishers

Closing the Inclusion Gap
Special and Mainstream Schools working in Partnership

Rita Cheminais

The future role of special schools as part of a progression towards inclusion is to act as launch pads for closer collaboration with mainstream schools. This book will help you to:

- organise and develop the consultancy role of special school staff
- plan inclusion training programmes for mainstream schools
- ensure that inclusive practice is on track with strategies for monitoring and evaluation
- market services to mainstream schools with time saving templates.
- manage dual placements

£16.00 • Paperback • 104 A4 pages • 1-84312-085-2 • Sept 2003

Language Development
Circle Time Sessions to Improve Communication Skills

Includes Video CD!

Marion Nash, Jackie Lowe and Tracey Palmer

By offering a pre-planned course of group sessions to cover an extended period of time, this book ensures that teachers cover the key areas when organising work to improve and develop children's language skills, thinking skills and emotional literacy. Included are

- a video CD containing an explanation and demonstration of the programme and its implementation, with comments from staff who have used it
- concise explanations of the terms and concepts involved
- clear guidelines for setting up and running the small group sessions
- structured lesson plans
- samples of assessment forms used
- photocopiable resources
- lists of further resources

It can be used with children from Nursery up to Key Stage 2.

£17.00 • Paperback • 144 A4 pages • 1-84312-156-5 • Sept 2003

Handbook for Pre-School SEN Provision
The Code of Practice in Relation to the Early Years

SECOND EDITION

Collette Drifte

From a review of the first edition: 'a useful publication for EPs with administrative responsibilities and for SEN officers.'
Education Psychology in Practice

Practitioners need to understand their responsibilities in light of the revised (2001) SEN Code of Practice. This book will help them to make appropriate provision for children with special educational needs – and feel confident that their paperwork is 'up to speed'. It provides practical guidance and a ready-made system for planning, monitoring and record keeping. It will:

- provide time-saving, photocopiable forms
- highlight good practice (and possible pitfalls) with case studies
- clarify the roles of professionals and agencies
- keep practitioners up to date with explanation of key concepts

£14.00 • Paperback • 96 A4 pages • 1-85346-837-1 • Sept 2003

A Handbook for Learning Support Assistants
Teachers and Assistants Working Together

SECOND EDITION

Glenys Fox

From a review of the first edition: '... a very useful book both for general interest and as a basic reader for those taking further qualifications in the area of classroom support.'
Managing Schools Today

Brought up to date with the 2001 Code of Practice and quality standards for TA training, this book ensures that:

- LSAs know what to expect of colleagues and colleagues know what to expect from LSAs
- children are given the best support possible by LSAs who understand the nature of their needs
- LSAs, teachers and SENCOs work together effectively to support the child with special needs
- training is relevant and helpful

£14.00 • Paperback • 104 A4 pages • 1-84312-081-X • Sept 2003

Appointing and Managing Learning Support Assistants
A Practical Guide for SENCOs and other Managers

Jennie George and Margaret Hunt

Written specially for SENCOs and other managers, this book offers guidance on employing and managing LSAs and all those who support children in mainstream education (LSAs, TAs, SSAs or STAs). The book includes

- photocopiable proformas to support staff recruitment and development
- how to make a focused response to audits using action plans
- what to expect from your LSAs
- suggestions on how to help teachers and LSAs communicate and share lesson plans
- advice for making the most of resources

This book will support SENCOs working in the early years, primary and secondary settings, head teachers and nursery managers.

£15.00 • Paperback • 80 A4 pages • 1-84312-062-3 • Sept 2003

Supporting Children with Special Educational Needs
A Guide for Assistants in Schools and Pre-schools

Marian Halliwell

Written in the context of recent legislation concerning disability and special educational needs, this practical guide contains helpful information about a range of special educational needs and provides clear guidance to help assistants give support in schools and pre-school settings.

The advice promotes the inclusion of all pupils and suggests ways to raise the achievement of every individual.

£15.00 • Paperback • 128 A4 pages • 1-84312-007-0 • Aug 2003

For more information, visit
www.fultonpublishers.co.uk

Access to the Curriculum

Curriculum Planning and Practical Activities for Pupils with Learning Difficulties

The Access to the Curriculum Series are practical guides to teaching subject areas of the National Curriculum; they highlight good practice, take into account the latest DfES guidance (such as the P Levels), offer help with planning teaching and learning objectives and give suggested lessons activities.

Written in plain English and full of ways to broaden pupil's learning experiences the books look at:

- the effective use of resources through good planning
- helping pupils meet individual targets that fit in with the P levels
- the work of City Learning Centres and how to use that expertise to meet specific needs

Access to ICT

Liz Singleton, Iain Ross and Liz Flavell

£14.00 • Paperback • 128 A4 pages • 1-84312-089-5 • November 2003

Access to Science

Claire Marvin and Chris Stokoe

£16.00 • Paperback • 168 A4 pages • 1-85346-917-3 • 2003

Access to Citizenship

Ann Fergusson and Hazel Lawson

£15.00 • Paperback • 136 A4 pages • 1-85346-910-6 • 2003

Activities for Children with Mathematical Learning Difficulties

Mel Lever

This short series of three books gives teachers and parents a range of ideas to help children with mathematical learning difficulties get to grips with mathematics. In order to help these children effectively, statements and teaching points need to be rephrased and produced in a variety of ways, using concrete and pictorial aids.

The activities in these books will help teachers to offer children a wide-ranging mathematical vocabulary – adding meaning to the words children already use rather than just adding words to their repertoire. These activities are flexible and can be used with children of a range of ages and ability levels, and in any order.

Measures and Handling Data

£12.00 • Paperback • 80 A4 pages • 1-85346-950-5 • 2003

Number

£12.00 • Paperback • 96 A4 pages • 1-85346-948-3 • 2003

Shape and Space

£12.00 • Paperback • 64 A4 pages • 1-85346-949-1 • 2003

Implementing Intensive Interaction in Schools

Guidance for Practitioners, Managers and Co-ordinators

Mary Kellett and **Melanie Nind**

By taking a detailed look at the implementation and management of Intensive Interaction, the authors of this book offer practical guidance on how to get the most from the approach in a school context.

They address a range of challenges across special, inclusive and ever-changing contexts.

£18.00 • Paperback • 216 pages • 1-84312-019-4 • May 2003

Gifted and Talented Children with Special Educational Needs

Double Exceptionality

Edited by **Diane Montgomery**

A NACE/FULTON PUBLICATION

'...likely to be of great value to teachers in special education, and other teachers as well, and of course psychologists, paediatricians, and in some cases psychiatrists and parents.'
Dr L F Lowenstein, Educational Psychologist

This practical text based on international research and practice enables the reader to identify highly able pupils with special needs and then make provision for them within the mainstream school.

£18.00 • Paperback • 224 A4 pages • 1-85346-954-8 • 2003

Creating a Responsive Environment for People with Profound and Multiple Learning Difficulties

SECOND EDITION

Jean Ware

'I certainly enjoyed this book. The wealth of examples made it easy to see how to move towards a more responsive environment for people with PMLD, and staff who embark upon using the text for a course are likely to find the experience rewarding. And ultimately, of course, people with PMLD will benefit from being with carers who have a better idea of how to encourage their development.'
Child Language Teaching and Therapy

£16.00 • Paperback • 144 pages • 1-85346-734-0 • 2003

Dragonfly Games: Developing and Supporting Dyslexic Learners 7-14

Sally Raymond

Dragonfly Games are designed for use with small groups of dyslexic pupils. These practical and varied resources can also be used outside of the classroom to encourage overlearning and revision of curriculum topics.

£14.00 • Paperback • 80 A4 pages
1-84312-038-0 • 2003

Educating Children with Acquired Brain Injury

Sue Walker and Beth Wicks

A child experiencing difficulties in school may be suffering from this 'hidden disability'. This book includes:

- education strategies that will enhance learning opportunities
- how to support the child experiencing social and emotional difficulties
- guidelines for working in partnership with families and other professionals
- a glossary of terms and a list of resources and useful organisations

£18.00 • Paperback • 128 pages • 1-84312-051-8 • December 2003

Including Children with Visual Impairment in Mainstream Schools
A Practical Guide

Pauline Davis

This book provides guidance to teachers, teaching assistants, service staff, parents and other professionals regarding the inclusion of children with visual impairments in mainstream primary schools. Materials for the whole school, small group and individual professional development are provided, and the framework of the book encourages critical reflection on the teaching practices, especially with regard to the inclusion of a child or children with visual impairments within mainstream primary schools.

£17.00 • Paperback • 144 A4 pages • 1-85346-914-9 • 2003

Dyslexia Included
A Whole School Approach

Edited by **Michael Thomson**

This practical book provides techniques and suggestions to help dyslexic pupils. Written by a team of experienced practitioners who work in a specialist school, it offers clear guidance and tried and tested strategies to help those who need support in this area.

£17.00 • Paperback • 112 A4 pages • 1-84312-002-X • 2003

Including Children 3 - 11 with Physical Disabilities
Practical Guidance for Mainstream Schools

Mark Fox

This guide helps early years and primary teachers, SENCOs, teaching assistants, parents of a child with a physical disability and other education professionals successfully include children with physical disabilities in mainstream classrooms.

£15.00 • Paperback • 176 pages • 1-85346-937-8 • 2003

Supporting Communication Disorders
A Handbook for Teachers and Teaching Assistants

Gill Thompson

This practical handbook provides SENCOs, class teachers and teaching assistants with a step-by-step guide to the identification of the possible causes of speech and language disorders, a basic knowledge of the underlying causes and guidance for developing strategies for support and intervention within the classroom.

£17.00 • Paperback • 96 A4 pages • 1-84312-030-5 • 2003

Special Educational Needs and School Improvement
Practical Strategies for Raising Standards

Jean Gross and **Angela White**

Providing a practical guide to strategic management in the field of special educational needs, this book gives the reader a framework for raising achievement throughout the school.

By focusing on how to manage SEN strategically, rather than on planning for individual children, this book shows how you can make it part of the overall school improvement process. It provides essential tools that SENCOs, head teachers and governors can use to analyse data, set objectives, measure and evaluate outcomes for SEN just as they do for other areas of the curriculum.

£17.00 • Paperback • 152 A4 pages • 1-84312-011-9 • May 2003

The SENCO Handbook
Working Within a Whole-School Approach

FOURTH EDITION

Elizabeth Cowne

This new edition includes:

- roles and responsibilities for schools in the light of the Revised Code of Practice (2001) and the Disability Discrimination Act Code of Practice for Schools (2002)
- planning IEPs within School Action and School Action Plus stages of the new graduated response
- working in partnership with parents and pupils
- strategies for planning an inclusive curriculum fro pupils with all levels of the National curriculum including the P levels
- managing effective support systems
- working with multi-professional networks
- a photocopiable activity pack for staff development

£19.00 • Paperback • 144 A4 pages • 1-84312-031-3 • 2003

Inclusive Education: Diverse Perspectives

Edited by **Melanie Nind, Kieron Sheehy, Katy Simmons** and **Jonathan Rix**

Drawing upon the experiences and practices of experts within the inclusive education sphere, this edited collection enables you to stay on top of current thinking, be in touch with inclusive education's past and keep abreast of its future development.

£17.00 • Paperback • 320 pages
1-84312-065-8 • Aug 2003

Inclusive Education:
Learners and Learning Contexts

Edited by **Melanie Nind, Kieron Sheehy** and **Katy Simmons**

This edited collection looks at:

- the impact gender, ethnicity, class and sexuality has on inclusive practice
- inclusive practice in different schools, different classrooms and beyond

£17.00 • Paperback • 304 pages • 1-84312-066-6 • Aug 2003

Published in association with

The Open University

Autistic Spectrum Disorders
Practical Strategies for Teachers and Other Professionals

Lynn Stuart, Jennie Beckwith, Amanda Cuthbertson, Rosamund Davison, Sue Grigor and Alison Howey

Increasingly, teachers are expected to identify problem areas and help children with ASD change or manage their behaviour appropriately. This book will help teachers to do that with off the shelf support including:

- helpful categorisation of problem areas for teachers to dip in and out of
- school specific solutions that will allow teachers to help children promptly and effectively
- advice on setting IEP targets
- photocopiable resources

£17.00 • Paperback • 144 A4 pages • 1-84312-155-7 • Nov 2003

Accessing the Curriculum for Pupils with Autistic Spectrum Disorders
Using the TEACCH Programme to Help Inclusion

Gary Mesibov and Marie Howley

£17.00 • Paperback • 144 A4 pages • 1-85346-795-2 • 2003

Moving On
Supporting Parents of Children with SEN

Alison Orphan

Written by a parent of children with SEN, this book tackles emotional as well as practical issues. It is a valuable, time-saving resource for anyone working with parent groups and contains material for ten group sessions. The book also includes:

- parent's handbook to supplement session plans
- personal anecdotes that highlight how parents feel in different situations
- photocopiable plans and handouts

For those working in Surestart projects, specialist settings, primary schools, EP services, counselling services and parent support organisations.

£15.00 • Paperback • 112 A4 pages • 1-84312-113-1 • Oct 2003

ORDER FORM

Qty	ISBN	Title	Price	Subtotal
	1-85346-910-6	Access to Citizenship	£15.00	
	1-84312-089-5	Access to ICT	£14.00	
	1-85346-917-3	Access to Science	£16.00	
	1-85346-795-2	Accessing the Curriculum for Pupils with ASDs	£17.00	
	1-84312-062-3	Appointing and Managing LSAs	£15.00	
	1-84312-155-7	Autistic Spectrum Disorders	£17.00	
	1-84312-085-2	Closing the Inclusion Gap	£16.00	
	1-85346-734-0	Creating a Responsive Environment ...	£16.00	
	1-84312-038-0	Dragonfly Games	£14.00	
	1-84312-002-X	Dyslexia Included	£17.00	
	1-84312-051-8	Educating Children with Acquired Brain Injury	£18.00	
	1-85346-954-8	Gifted and Talented Children with SEN	£18.00	
	1-84312-081-X	Handbook for Learning Support Assistants	£14.00	
	1-85346-837-1	Handbook for Pre-School SEN Provision	£14.00	
	1-84312-019-4	Implementing Intensive Interaction in Schools	£18.00	
	1-85346-937-8	Including Children 3 - 11 with Physical Dis.	£15.00	
	1-85346-914-9	Including Children with VI in Mainstream Schools	£17.00	
	1-84312-065-8	Inclusive Ed.: Diverse Perspectives	£17.00	
	1-84312-066-6	Inclusive Ed.: Learners & Learning Contexts	£17.00	
	1-84312-156-5	Language Development (with video CD)	£17.00	
	1-85346-950-5	Measures and Handling Data	£12.00	
	1-84312-113-1	Moving On	£15.00	
	1-85346-948-3	Number	£12.00	
	1-84312-031-3	SENCO Handbook	£19.00	
	1-85346-949-1	Shape and Space	£12.00	
	1-84312-011-9	SEN & School Improvement	£17.00	
	1-84312-007-0	Supporting Children with SENs	£15.00	
	1-84312-030-5	Supporting Communication Disorders	£17.00	

Postage and Packing: £2.75 for up to 2 books, plus 50p for each book thereafter. Maximum carriage charge £8.00. Orders of 24 or more books post free. Approximate prices (indicated by 'c') are subject to change on publication.

P&P	
TOTAL	

Please complete delivery details

Name: ....

Organisation: ....

....

Address: ....

....

....

....

....

Postcode:. ....

Tel: ....

To order
Send to:
David Fulton Publishers,
Freepost LON16469
London W4 5BR

Freephone: 0500 618 052
Fax: 020 8996 3622

☐ Please send me a copy of your complete catalogue

☐ Please send me email updates on your new books

Email: ....

www.fultonpublishers.co.uk

Payment

☐ Please invoice (applicable to schools, LEAs and other institutions)

☐ I enclose a cheque payable to David Fulton Publishers Ltd *(include postage and packing)*

☐ Please charge to my credit card (Visa/Barclaycard, Access/Mastercard, American Express, Switch, Delta)

card number ☐☐☐☐ ☐☐☐☐ ☐☐☐☐ ☐☐☐☐ ☐☐☐☐

expiry date ☐☐☐☐

(Switch customers only) valid from ☐☐☐☐ issue number ☐☐